UP CLOSE

DINOSAURS

HEATHER AMERY

W
FRANKLIN WATTS

Published in 2007 by Franklin Watts
Reprinted in 2010

Copyright © 2007 Arcturus Publishing Limited

Franklin Watts
338 Euston Road
London NW1 3BH

Franklin Watts Australia
Level 17/207 Kent Street
Sydney, NSW 2000

Author: Heather Amery
Editor (new edition): Ella Fern
Designers (new edition): Steve West, Steve Flight

Picture credits: Ardea: 5 top, 15 top, 17, 18 top; Discovery Communications Inc: 16, 19; Natural History Museum (London): front and back cover, title page, 2, 3, 4, 5 bottom, 6, 7, 8 top, bottom, 9, 10, 11 top, 12, 13 top, bottom, 14, 15 bottom, 20, 21, 23; Science Photo Library: 11 bottom, 18 bottom.

A CIP catalogue record for this book is available from the British Library

Dewey number: 567.9

ISBN: 978-1-4451-0130-9
SL000939EN

Printed in China

Franklin Watts is a division of Hachette Children's Books, an Hachette UK Company
www.hachette.co.uk

Contents

Millions and millions of years before any people lived on Earth, the world belonged to the dinosaurs! Some were as small as a chicken. Others were longer than three buses in a row. From the knee-high to the sky-high, dinosaurs ruled the Earth for about 160 million years.

DINOSAUR DAYS

The earliest dinosaurs lived during the Triassic period. Then came the Jurassic period, with dinosaurs like the meat-eater *Allosaurus* (al-oh-SORE-us). After that was the Cretaceous period that was, sadly, the end of the line for the dinosaurs.

EMPTY NESTERS

Like most reptiles, dinosaurs hatched from eggs. Some fossils show that certain dinosaurs may have been very protective of their young, like the plant-eater *Maiasaura* (MY-ah-SORE-ah). It guarded its babies and brought them food.

Dominated

DIG IT

When most dinosaurs died, their bodies just rotted away. But if the conditions were right, the bones would turn to stone. These ancient remains are called fossils.

Scientists believe that there are hundreds of dinosaur species yet to be found.

5

Mighty Meat-

C arnivorous (meat-eating) dinosaurs were the most fearsome. They all had the same favourite meal—MEAT. When their dagger-like, flesh-ripping teeth fell out, new ones grew to take their place. No dentures for these dudes!

We can find out what dinosaurs ate by studying fossils.

RUN FOR YOUR LIFE!

Some of the most dangerous dinosaurs were small but speedy. *Deinonychus* (die-NON-i-kus) was only 3 metres long, but fast and fierce, with savage claws.

Eaters

ARMED AND DANGEROUS

Allosaurus was the top predator of the Jurassic Period. It had a powerful tail, three claws on each hand, and jagged teeth perfect for tearing flesh.

The great meat-eater *Megalosaurus* (MEG-ah-loh-**SORE**-us) was the first dinosaur ever to be named.

FOOD FIGHTS

Carnivorous dinosaurs sometimes attacked other dinosaurs. In Mongolia's Gobi Desert, the bones of a meat-eating *Velociraptor* (vel-O-si-RAP-tor) and the bones of a plant-eating *Protoceratops* (pro-toe-SER-a-tops) were found together. The two had fought to the death.

Herbivores: Gentle Giants?

T he biggest creatures that have ever walked the Earth were the herbivorous (plant-eating) dinosaurs. Just the neck of *Mamenchisaurus* (mah-MEN-chee-SORE-us) measured 11 metres long—the length of a school bus! The plant-eaters went looking for food, not trouble, so other dinosaurs had little to fear from them. But if attacked, they put up a fight!

VICIOUS VEGGIE

Brachiosaurus (brak-ee-oh-SORE-us) was as heavy as a dozen elephants. It was too massive to move fast. But it had a thick and powerful tail to keep off attackers.

SPIKY FELLOW

The strange-looking *Stegosaurus* (STEG-oh-SORE-us) had a row of triangular plates down its back. Paleontologists (people who study prehistoric life) think it may have turned the plates to face the sun, soaking in rays to warm its body.

Poor *Stegosaurus'* brain was smaller than any other dinosaur's.

Some plant-eating dinosaurs may have swallowed stones to help grind up their food. Yum!

TOUGH LOVE

The plant-eating *Pachycephalosaurus* (PAK-ee-SEF-a-loh-SORE-us) was a real bonehead! The solid dome on the top of its skull was 25 cm thick.

BACK OFF!

This dinosaur, the *Triceratops* (try-SER-a-tops) looks a bit like a modern-day rhinoceros. Since it was a strict veggie, its three horns were not used for hunting, but for defence against its enemies.

Tyrannosaurus:

When you hear the word "dinosaur," who comes to mind first? Bet you said *T. rex*! *Tyrannosaurus rex* (tie-RAN-oh-SORE-us REX), was definitely one of the biggest, hungriest, and fiercest meat-eating dinosaurs. Its name means "king of the tyrant lizards".

SCAVENGER
Because of its huge bulk and short arms, *T. rex* may not have been a great hunter. Mostly, it just ate the remains of prey left by other carnivores!

Dino King

T. rex's arms were so short that they couldn't even touch each other!

ALL THE BETTER TO EAT YOU WITH

Tyrannosaurus rex had a head as long as a fridge. It could have opened its jaws wide enough to swallow a man in one gulp. Curved, jagged teeth, longer than a human's hand, could puncture the organs of its prey before tearing it apart.

BIG BULLIES

T. Rex was one of the biggest meat-eating dinosaurs. But we now know that other carnivores, like *Giganotosaurus* (JI-gah-NO-tuh-SORE-us) were even bigger!

While dinosaurs roamed the Earth, equally awesome beasts ruled the seas. These prehistoric sea monsters evolved from land reptiles and adapted to life in the water. They still had to come to the surface of the water to breathe between dives, like whales and dolphins do.

LURKING

Sea monster sightings have been reported all over the world. The most famous 'mythical' monster is Scotland's Loch Ness Monster.

Fossils suggest that *Ichthyosaurs* didn't lay eggs but gave birth to live young.

BIG FISH

Ichthyosaurs (IKH-thee-oh-sores) looked a lot like modern-day dolphins—but they were much, *much* bigger. They zipped through the water as fast as 40 km per hour.

DOWN IN THE DEPTHS

With their skinny necks and roly-poly bodies, *Plesiosaurs* (PLE-see-oh-sores) looked awkward, but their paddle-like flippers helped them twist and turn in the water.

Fearsome Fliers

In prehistoric times reptiles filled the skies too. The *Pterosaurs* (Teh-ruh-**SORES**) were flying reptiles— some as small as birds, others as big as aeroplanes!

SCOOPER
Pteranodon (Ter-RANN-oh-don) would skim through the water, scoop up fish, and swallow them whole.

17

FINALLY-FEATHERS!

Archeopteryx (ark-ee-OP-ter-iks) is the first flying reptile known to have had feathery wings. It had claws on its wings, which it may have used to climb trees.

With wings up to 12 metres across, *Quetzalcoatlus* (kwet-zal-co-AT-lus) was the largest creature ever to sail the skies.

WINGING IT

At about 70 cm long, Microraptor [MY-cro-RAP-tor] was not big in dinosaur terms. But it had four wings—two at the front, and two feathery back legs which it could use to help glide through the air.

AIR-VOLUTION

Rhamphorynchus (RAM-foh-RIN-khus), one of the early pterosaurs, had spiky teeth great for spearing fish. Later flying reptiles like *Quetzalcoatlus* looked quite different. They had much shorter tails but longer necks.

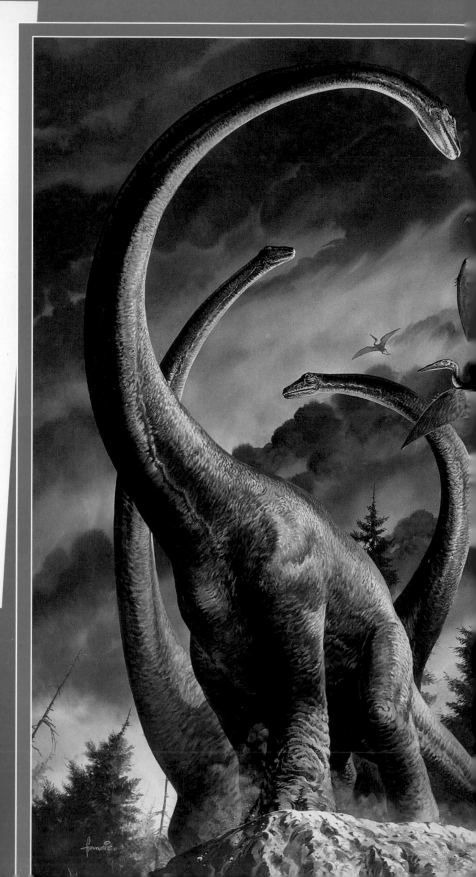

T he dinosaurs ruled the Earth for 165 million years. But 65 million years ago, they all disappeared. What happened? Did one catastrophic event wipe them out, or did they gradually become extinct?

VOLCANOES

Erupting volcanoes may have spewed so much lava and poisonous gas into the air that the dinosaurs couldn't survive.

Disappear

LIGHTS OUT

A massive meteorite—more than 9 km wide—may have crashed down on Earth, causing dust to block out the sun. The dinosaurs might have frozen in the cold!

COLD SPELL

A less dramatic explanation is that Earth's climate changed gradually. The weather got drier and cooler, and the dinosaurs just couldn't handle the chill.

There is another strange theory about what may have happened to the dinosaurs. Some people think that space aliens carried them away. What do you think?

Glossary

Carnivore
An animal that eats meat.

Cretaceous Period
The third and final period of the dinosaurs (142–65 million years ago).

Fossil
The impression of an ancient plant or animal that is preserved in stone.

Herbivore
An animal that only eats plants.

Ichthyosaurs
Large prehistoric reptiles with fins who lived in the sea.

Jurassic Period
The second period of the dinosaurs (206–142 million years ago).

Lava
Magma that flows out of volcanoes when they erupt.

Meteorite
A rock or metal object from space that has collided with the Earth.

Paleontologist
Someone who studies fossils and prehistoric life.

Plesiosaurs
Thin-bodied prehistoric reptiles with flippers who lived in the sea.

Predator
An animal (a carnivore) that hunts and eats other animals.

Prehistoric
From the time before recorded history began.

Pterosaurs
Flying prehistoric reptiles.

Reptile
A cold-blooded vertebrate (animal with a backbone), covered in scales or a horny plate. Reptiles include lizards, snakes, crocodiles and turtles.

Triassic Period
The earliest period of the dinosaurs (248–206 million years ago).

Further Reading

Dinosaur
John Malam, Dorling Kindersley
(Experience series), 2006

Dinosaur (Ultimate Sticker Book)
Dorling Kindersley, 2004

Dinosaurs
Stephanie Turnbull, Usborne (Beginners
series), 2003

**Dinosaurs! The Biggest Baddest
Strangest Fastest**
Howard Zimmerman, Atheneum, 2000

The Ultimate Book of Dinosaurs
Dougal Dixon, Ticktock Publishing, 2005

Index